The Second Thing I Remember

A COLLECTION OF POEMS BY

JUDITH HOUGEN

Judith Hougen

Minnesota Voices Project Number 56

NEW RIVERS PRESS 1993

Library of Congress Catalog Card Number 92-64071
ISBN 0-89823-143-4

Edited by David Cline and C. W. Truesdale
Editorial Assistance by Paul J. Hintz
Cover Painting by Dale R. Johnson
Book Design and Typesetting by Peregrine Publications

The publication of *The Second Thing I Remember* has been made possible by generous grants from the Jerome Foundation and the Metropolitan Regional Arts Council (from an appropriation by the Minnesota Legislature). Additional support has been provided by the First Bank System Foundation, Liberty State Bank, the National Endowment for the Arts (with funds appropriated by the Congress of the United States), the Star Tribune/Cowles Media Company, the Tennant Company Foundation, the United Arts Fund, and the contributing members of New Rivers Press. New Rivers Press also wishes to acknowledge the Minnesota Non-Profits Assistance Fund for its invaluable support.

New Rivers Press books are distributed by:

The Talman Company
131 Spring Street, Suite 201 E-N
New York NY 10012

Bookslinger
2402 University Avenue West
Saint Paul MN 55114

The Second Thing I Remember has been manufactured in the United States of America for New Rivers Press, 420 N. 5th Street/Suite 910, Minneapolis, MN 55401 in a first edition of 1,200 copies.

For my parents, brother, and sister
with love and gratitude

To Michael—
Hope these poems find
a home with you—
I enjoyed talking
with you! Thanks—
Judy
March 1995

Acknowledgements

Some of the poems in *The Second Thing I Remember* have previously appeared in the following publications: "Summer on Lake Minnetonka" and "Bebop Down to the Car Wash Boogie," in *Great River Review*; "Muscles Hougen Comes Out of Softball Retirement" in *Tar River Poetry*; "She Spoke of Tomatoes" in *CutBank*; "Why the Young Girl Dreams of Horses" in *The Georgia Review*; "Flagman, Northeast Montana" in *Kansas Quarterly*; "Coming of Age" in *Bottomfish*; "This Town that Takes the Series" in *Indiana Review*; and "Home of the Brave" in *The Perimeter of Light: Writing About the Vietnam War* (New Rivers Press, 1992). Our thanks to the editors of these publications for allowing us to reprint the poems here.

"China Letters," "The Origin of Tigers," "The Story of Math," and "This Town that Takes the Series" originally appeared in *The Origin of Tigers: An Anthology of Poetry and Creative Prose, Selections by the Winners of the 1990 Loft-McKnight Writers Awards and Awards of Distinction*, published by the Loft, 1990.

The author would like to thank the Loft and the McKnight Foundation for sponsoring the Loft-McKnight Award, which provided invaluable resources and encouragement in the production of this manuscript. Thanks also to the Poetry Hostages (a.k.a. Carol Light, Ricki Thompson, Suzanne Swanson, Tracy Youngblom, and Kathy Whitcomb-Nelson) for good ideas, support, and all that Diet Dr. Pepper. And, last, the author wishes to extend a special thanks to Deborah Keenan for her great generosity of time, spirit, and expertise that inspired and guided the formation of this book.

Contents

III. THE LAST SPILL OF LIGHT

IV. THE LENGTH OF THE WORLD AS WE KNOW IT

Between Earth and the Closest Star

A NEW WAY TO SEE THIS SIMPLE,
ENDLESS FIELD OF MY LIFE.

The Origin of Tigers

In the beginning, the sun's hands were
vacant and its heat could host nothing
else. The earth was not green,
but the unbearable orange of an immense
iron left in the coals for centuries.
So, the sun reached slowly back
into itself, easing to a stop
when the first animal appeared
in the feathery ash, though
its body was branded with the last,
retracting flame, the only legacy
of the first earth. Every night
he dreamed of perfect fire
and sometimes standing in the warm,
brilliant light there was a strangely
colored memory he could only compare
to the hot, crimson taste in the open
belly of a surprised gazelle. This is why
poetry exists, to tell the origin of tigers,
to always remember for them one detail
of heaven, that fiery meat which feeds us.

The Story of Math

I've been thinking about infinity, this afternoon
dividing 5 by 3 and getting 1.6666666, a Niagara
of numbers bursting the side door of the calculator,
spilling out of my hand onto the floor, unending.
My mother came home, "You've been playing with
the calculator again haven't you? For God's sake,
get a mop." What I mean is, I've been realizing how
much my mind is limited to eight digit display, ready
to admit I haven't the strength to carry the 2
very far. Infinity is a woman of unbearable light
and because so many of us weep to touch her,
she sent her 10 beautiful and mysterious children
into our lives: the stoical faces of 5s, laughing 9s,
military 7s, hardassed 8s, all gathering now to sleep
in the bottomless field of a summer night. Even
the distance between earth and the closest star
is too much to apprehend. Alone in the back yard
tonight, I can bridge only 5 feet, 3 inches of the gap,
like the first 8 digits of something endless, wet grass
cooling the soles of my feet, the incalculable smell
of apricots ripening above my head in the dark.

The Second Thing I Remember

In the Alaskan town where I was born, there was a man
who plowed the streets after each snow. Before starting,
he would phone his wife to be sure his son was home
safe. The one time he neglected to call, the boy was tunneling
in a snow bank beside a road and was killed. This is a true
story. Snow in his mouth, snow in his pockets, his chest
crushed. None of us knew the man or the boy and we moved
away soon after this. But I think of it during a hard snow
when my car creeps down the highway, the windshield blurring
with ice. And also early the next morning when the plow
lumbering past my house scrapes me from sleep, the harsh
metal raking asphalt, headlights passing just above
my head. He stands there in the darkest room of winter.
I don't know what this boy wants. I have done all I can do.
I have brought in lanterns, blankets, I have shouted warnings
in my sleep. I have tried to build this poem for his rescue,
but there is so much snow I cannot lift it alone or pry
away the top layer in time to let him escape. It is always
too late and when I awaken, I am first aware my arms
feel heavy like ice and I remember I have no children.

Horror Stories

Becky Huie told the one about
the honeymooners with car trouble
done in by the wandering murderer like she
knew them personally. Eleven years to my eight,
Becky knew about these things, she had

been around. In the backyard magnolia,
our legs braced between
limbs, I shifted positions, the edge
of the woodpile became two logs more than
wood, maniacs grew in the hedgerows

in the same proportion as darkness changed
hands with light. In the daytime, I was in
the third grade in Falls Church, Virginia, and my
father worked at the Pentagon. He knew secrets
and couldn't leave the country. We drove into D.C.

occasionally. I was afraid to descend the stairs
at the Lincoln Memorial, the white steps pulling me
away from the edge. If you fell down, they could
kill you three or four times. Sometimes, I begged
my father for a secret, just one, wondering

what kind of story was big enough to scare
a whole country, lock shut the borders. I thought
of this stepping down the white stones,
stories tangled in dark branches, my legs
trembling slightly, holding my father's hand.

Why the Young Girl Dreams of Horses

At meadow edge, fetlocks dressed
in jonquil and shooting star, he shakes the proud
trumpet of his head and gallops
the girl to the other side of her life.
The black mane cracking with wind
is a ribbon he offers the girl
shining between clutched fingers. His shoulder
muscles rumble up bone like dark
fists in a new rhythm that percussions
her shins hard against packed ribs.
The girl's cheek burrows against the stallion's
neck, listening to the strum of wrist-thick
tendons pulse like a mallet
in her ear, pounding her into
a music she's never before heard. In the sun,
his moist muzzle gleams, it is enough the warm
voice of the wind in her mouth, her hair snapping
back like a banner from her neck. Soon,
with knees still wobbling in time to the ride,
she will ease down from the saddle, the smell
of leather wound around her hand, and her feet
will dance in one unsteady moment upon
earth now singing the flute of her body.

Coming of Age

We skidded up in late afternoon to the lake cottage,
hot, steel bucket in the back seat bulging
with wild strawberries, the cologne of July
blown in our hair. Engine off, the day
squeezed close again like the sweaty arms of my old aunt.
The women buzzed the bucket to the kitchen in a rush
of blue aprons. My nails, hemmed with russet horseshoes,
dug out hulls, while my mother's voice
rose clear as the scent of fresh tablecloths
snapped open in the dining room. After dinner,
the berries waded in heavy cream, we relaxed
in a humid breeze barely breathing off Lake Minnetonka,
the sky sinking into a last cup of lukewarm coffee.
At twelve, time reinventing my body, I was old enough
to sit amid the tribe in poppy-print dresses
and red-faced toenails. From our patch of porch light,
I heard waves slapping thc shore, realized
even darkness is comforted by the talk of women,
the sweetness raised in the pink lines of their hands.

She Spoke of Tomatoes

June, they'd arrive in the driveway
jungled in the trunk
yawned up to divulge a hundred
dumbfounded flowers
suddenly famous with light.
Mother pounded down stakes,
smiling, shredding
a loud daisy print dress
worn ten years ago.
Drenching holes all afternoon,
she smoothed out the roots in mud.
By July, they'd punched out,
fists that woke hard and green in her palm.
Mid-summer brought a ritual morning hosing,
souping each plant till cracked ground
remembered again how to drink.
Come August,
tomatoes lit up the kitchen counter,
gorgeous redheads scattered sexy
at her elbow, picked
when ripeness most approaches speech,
when her low garden whispering
swelled to a perfect answer.
They were mother's pumped-up
opinion of summer,
a private conversation rowed
on the brown windowsill,
what she and the sunlight
said to each other.

What She Meant Was

I was fifteen and visiting my grandmother
for the last time. She knew enough

to pucker her lips slightly
when I lowered my face, dutifully,

in front of her son and daughter-in-law—
my mother—who loved her like her own

mother and lived with her during
the Korean War when my father

became a collection of vague
lines scrawled from a country

full of nightmares. Drinking coffee
at evening around the kitchen table,

they spoke about lists for market
tomorrow, the next air mail package,

but not about me yet
or my siblings. It was too early

and they were still so afraid for him.
She had said, *if this is the end, I hope it comes*

quickly, and what she meant was, the dying is
the only fearful part. I leaned my face

over hers for a last difficult kiss,
allowing the distances to fully bloom

between us. It never occurred to me then
how it is our lives rise up out of each other,

terrible and wondrous. The cancer had
dismantled her quick enough, my brother,

sister, and I turned for the door, our eyes
signaling each other in one accord:

let this be over. The door opened
to a swell of noise, air studded

with light. Turning down
the hall, like three centers of stillness,

we walked back to our lives, slowly, without fear.

Points of No Return

This is the year Elvis dies and Delavan, Wisconsin, finally
gets a Pizza Hut and I'm working another summer scooping up
ice cream at Lake Lawn Lodge just before my senior year.

I scratch out rhymes on the back of placemats between customers
and on a half hour break write my first bad poem about loss.
My mother packs me dinners, making sure one of my two aprons

is clean, though inevitably faint stains map the cloth
like the outlines of ghostly continents. I can throw together
five banana splits without blinking. The trick is to peel

and slice the fruit before you flip in ice cream. It'll melt
less. That table tipped me a dollar for the effort. It's a slow August
afternoon and Marge, the cashier, announces Elvis is dead

in a voice that sounds so monumental I'm surprised I feel
nothing. Within days, the number of roadside velvet painting
concessions shoots up like weeds with different Elvis poses,

varying sneers. I want to write a poem about it: *each one*
a billboard for death and *middle-aged women maundering*
(my new word) *among the portraits like headstones.* This is

the year I dream about college in Minneapolis, loving
and hating Delavan, Wisconsin, the way every kid loves and hates
a small town they are about to outgrow, not knowing what to term

the ambivalence, not understanding the signs, how points of no
return are so effortless you can't mark them until after the door
is shut. The ice cream parlor closes at ten and I mop up counters,

gray dishrag coaxing chrome spiggots to shine before it all
starts again. I think about Elvis occasionally since Marge
is in mourning and about the hysterical fans run over at his funeral.

In seventeen years, I have never known a desperate passion
that makes you leave yourself like that. I report for work six days
a week, keep my uniform clean, tolerate tourists from Chicago.

But it is all the edge of something, some place I need to go mapped
out on the poem folded in my apron pocket, ticket to a destination
I can't even picture, a new way to see this simple, endless field of my life.

Straddling the Headwaters with my Grandfather, Itasca, Minnesota, 1968

1.
One of three kids crazy to be out of the car at last,
I stood with a foot on each bank of the Mississippi,
three feet wide at the headwaters, like a giant who could
crush Minneapolis and St. Paul, 200 miles downstream,
with my feet, long as a city block. In my dutch boy
haircut and culotte outfit, I posed with the family in front
of the teepee with the bored Indian in native dress.
The older man, half-stranger who wandered through
a handful of my life, stood by, trying to be nice to me.

2.
Grandfather, you divorced your wife through the mail
after the war and then wanted to buy me postcards in
the Itasca State Park gift shop twenty-two years later.
You were uncomfortable. I had difficulty concentrating
on which ones to choose. I think I left empty-handed.

3.
I washed the beautiful granite stones in the stream
and thought, *in a month this water will be in Louisiana.*
I wanted to launch a delicate glass bottle that would discover
the warm arms of the Gulf, startling jellyfish, pink stomachs
of the sea. There would be a message in it: *My name is Judy.*
I sent this from Minnesota. Here is my address. Can we be friends?

4.
I can't remember anything you said that day. It was getting
late, the peanut butter sandwiches gone. My mother
was the good fairy of peace, cleaning the picnic table clutter,
dissolving arguments, moving like a flock of sparrows. It was
a long drive home. I knew so little, I wanted to ask, *what is
the rest of the story? What does it mean to love you?* Instead,
I napped, my head trembling against the darkness of the window.

5.
I note my physical distance from you in the photographs.
My eight-year-old face worried the world would swallow my
parents and leave me to be raised by my own insecurities.
When you die alone ten years from now, I will ask myself what I
should feel. In the beginning, the water's path
is ankle deep. Soon after, the terrible traction,
momentum of water, takes over, capable of lighting a city.
The distance splitting the banks is impossible.
Grandfather, think of the years this way. You see how quickly it
becomes too late. The current between has already drowned us.

Poem for My Father, Painting the Living Room

He loves the quiet reason of
the brush sizzling down the wall
and the tiny smacks of the roller
furred a brilliant white. Perhaps
the cleanness attracts him.
The morning of wiping away. His one
ear has finally gone deaf from
the wars, hours of mortar, the one
sound that said you were alive.
He catches low tones the best.
But today, he works alone, a loud
transistor radio scratching the air.
The previous white is giving way,
nearly gray in comparison. His brush
melts into the shining pail,
he does the job carefully, never
thinking about the futility of white,
how willingly it opens itself.
He rinses each tool methodically,
the smell of new paint will drift
in the house for days, but already it is
absorbing all the harms of our living.

Summer on Lake Minnetonka

We put out in old Uncle Howard's pontoon boat
with a canary canvas roof.
I grabbed the rail, my neck swallowed
by an orange life preserver.
The boat chopped frothy caps,
I glanced back —
the cabin, Bredeson Point,
that late summer greenery merged
into one long mess of shore.
I crouched down by one side of the boat,
letting plowed slats of water
kick at my fingers.

My younger sister and I stood
ankle deep in lake, motionless,
minnows scooting around
our great silent toes
or coaxing surface with midget mouths.
Clean peanut butter jars held wide,
we swooped like kingfishers.
"Judy, I got one!," she cried.
Uncle Howard allowed a nickel a dozen.
Unconcerned, they sashayed
in cloudy water, shining past
my glass magnified thumb.

I plopped potato salad on my plate,
piled like the eroding stones
lining the point.
Older cousins disdained picnics
and littered Bredeson's dock, edging

toward bronzedom. My older brother,
thirteen and glandular,
lay buried in the fraying hammock
eyeing the underwear ads
in the *Ladies Home Journal.*
Bob Bredeson strolled over,
waiting a new load of rock
to slow the eternal ransacking.

Bass, northern, walleye.
Daylight, 1969, my sister
and I hold humble poles,
baskets meager with perch and sunfish,
dreaming of a meaty tug.
At dusk, grandaddy northern hit,
whacking us with water
as I strained him to surface,
a spit up burst of beast,
spine fins spiked
out, tail hacking air,
reswallowing lake, indignant,
jaws jerking line, snapping off
the bamboo tip of my rod.
My sister ran off the dock shrieking
and wouldn't swim for a week.

Uncle Howard
paid two hundred thousand
to remodel his cabin two years
before brain cancer.
Last time I saw him,

half his head was bandaged, safety pins
holding the bows of his glasses
over mummified ears, hoisting
up a clumsy smile,
the old dance of his long
hands adjusting
the pontoon's skewed canopy.

At evening, Mother ferreted out her kids,
found me in my grass-kneed jeans,
brown feet in P. F. Flyers,
fingers carefully tightening
around pancake rocks
skittering black on Minnetonka.
As her hand nuzzled into mine,
chill air sifted over
salty skin. Past evening,
the lake becomes a dark field,
somewhere a fish slapped breathless
into stars, but it was too early
for loss, we navigated
toward the single porch light.

The Given Story

I drop by late. Mom leaves a note: *green beans and ham in the fridge if you're hungry.* The beans are sitting in their open Super Valu can, heaven knows how long, a side dish of tetanus waiting to happen. I'll eat them anyway, wondering why it is our parents are always trying to kill us and why it is we let them. As children, we'd fly around the back end of the paneled station wagon, the three of us potential hood ornaments, seatbelts buried from day one. Then there were those silver cake decorating BB balls Mom let us eat by the handful. When I was twenty-three I read the label: *Decoration only. Not meant for consumption.* Lord, they were covered with real metal. I'm amazed I made it through airports. How did any of us ever grow up? I snap on the TV news, one tragedy leaning against another. It's the missing boy again. I think we all had guardian angels back then. This new generation is fragile—every parental move crucial, a rope tightening around the word yes. They take all these precautions, but the boy seemed old enough to go to the convenience store to rent a video one evening last October. His mother is on the screen, resembling an old woman now and I scrutinize her like the nosy next door neighbor who always hangs around, managing to say the wrong thing. I imagine how good his homecoming would be—the boy reappearing suddenly, smelling like wet leaves, his mother's tears solid on his cheek. I'm thinking of my endless chases with neighbor kids summer nights and the time I decided to walk back to our old house and a stranger brought me home before my parents even knew I was missing. It seemed darkness was an open hand where children breathed forever. This is the story I've been given. But his mother could easily be my own, though older, of course, by this time, the lines the incident scrawled into her face softened by two decades now. She would no longer repeat *if only* when she first awakens and her senses surface, but wonder occasionally what her daughter would be doing at twenty-nine, what's important to her. The cool ham is ringed with a thin, white line of fat and the beans collapse next to it, steaming. The startled toast hops from its small inferno. I'm hungry for all of it. I remember a short grace, salt the food, begin to eat my meal.

Singing the Simple Pearls

THE NUMBERS INSIDE DON'T END,
THEY, NEVER, NEVER END . . .

Once upon a Time

The love poem I cannot write comes
this October and you have no part
of these maples, their hands stained
by the cold, alone with the fist
of my heart, trembling together
for warmth. All summer,
the leaves believed they were stars,
this was their story,
until the bluster to hard ground
where the noisy confetti
of kicked-up oak leaves
sounds a crowded stadium shouting
rushing, rushing, rushing and you and I
boost to our feet amid toppled cocoa
cheering for love and victory.
But in the spilled paint
of alders, I am alone, my feet
swishing comfort to the empty constellations
of elms: *listen, sleep, listen.* I rummage
through the ruckus of mountain ash
because no other color
can rouse a thousand paper mouths
to ask, *where, where are you now?*
Once upon a time in early morning,
the first good frost spilled
a million new stars across galaxies
of icy leaves. The leaves finally spoke: they said
love can be a gift winter brings, shining
patiently all night on cedar and black walnut.
Think of it, after the cold, a beauty
burned into us suddenly, crystalized
like the beginning of a story:
once upon a time
against our small and separate skies . . .

Octoberfest at the N.P., Missoula, 1988

The German beer is the color of standing water
in November, too bitter, but this is a celebration,
so I order one more. The rim of my glass is cool
under my lips in this night air, the Big Sky Mudflaps
playing "Shake, Rattle and Roll" at the Northern Pacific

train depot turned restaurant. I'm standing near
the tracks talking to Diana about location: *geography*
is overrated, mobility isn't everything—easy for me
to say, I'm leaving. I know she's remembering the mornings
in Germany, the wild crosscountry trip to Missoula years

before I knew her. I think I'm consoling the weight
of marriage, work, family, those anchors of our later lives.
Now, the Burlington Northern rattles by, the long whistle
trailing like an immense ribbon, ruffling the amber

in our glasses. That noise awakened me all summer at
four or five in the morning. *What is it? The alarm clock?*
my senses finally surfaced. *No, just the train.* Then I
submerged again before work at the grocery. During college
in St. Paul, years ago, Teresa wanted to jump a freight

train, usually just before finals. I think she would've done
it if I'd said yes. She wanted to be rocked to sleep,
slip into that steady clacking, the dark shine of the rails
and wake with the sun blasting her face in Rochester or
Des Moines. My last hurrah in Missoula, Montana, beer

I can barely drink, hundreds of people in chilly air
creating a collective sweater against the impending cold,
the sax winding down like a siren after an emergency—
the best night I'll have all fall and after the move nothing
like it for a long, long time. Diana has a daughter she loves,

but feels guilty for owning a color TV, so she loans it to
everyone she knows. Maybe she sees my life as an open door
and envies me. Perhaps leaving is a door I'll regret.
When the band quits at one and we leave the haloes
of light, we both walk to our cars, enter separate darknesses.
Fumbling for that familiar key, we find our own way home.

Bebop Down to the Car Wash Boogie

Yeah, Mary, early April and seventy cloudless perfecta-
mundo degrees in your '69 Olds 98 you haven't so much as
spit on since October, cruising down to the All American
Auto Wash like it was Mecca on a Friday afternoon with
Dan Seals singing, *I'm not after your body*
baby, I just want you to dance with me, so sin-
cere you about kiss the radio. You are the biggest
dancing fool I know, Mary, doing the Lindy down
to the All American Auto Wash with crooning Dan and
me in mirror shades doing back up passenger-side.
What else can we do? This cowboy wants to
bop with you baby all night long, I want to
bebop with you baby till the break of dawn.
Bumping down Brooks, we screech up into the Auto Wash drive-
way by the high powered (yeow!) vacuum for the simple
subtraction of paths of crumbs and smushed boxes
we've stomped on all winter or lost beneath the seat:
Better Cheddars, Nilla Wafers, Cracker Jack, Cap'N
Crunch, Ding Dong wrappers and three dozen Diet
Pepsi cans. Like those German kids who left a clever trail,
we've driven our way back from zero to the car wash
line. Radio up another notch, sunning on the hood,
legs crossed, white bone of our ankles waggling
to so much music. Mary, this day adds clear up
to infinity. Believe me, the numbers
inside don't end, they never, never end,
we could spend our lives trying to count this high.

Flagman, Northeast Montana

Quarter mile from jackhammers
jamming blunt iron into old highway,
breaking up hunks of asphalt,
your sign seesaws in gusts
out to blast everything this morning.
Your options are clear:
SLOW, STOP—warnings, that's all,
with ten bucks an hour for bad arches
and all the boredom you can stand.
Between cars you can look
straight into Canada, Saskatchewan
lining the north horizon,
the spine of other lives.
Even the name, *Saskatchewan,*
is a mysterious curse
you shout to yourself.
The wind rattles your clothes
battering the spaces between shirt and skin
until you can't think anymore.
You learn the hard grasp
and teeter of the warning pole,
wait the next car's
deceleration into your life,
consider your choices,
readable from a long way off.

Encounter

We buried you four years ago.
It was a dream. Four years.
But the large, open hands,
eyes that could hold anything,
it was you.

The encounter is this: David,
I saw you standing there,
talking, laughing, so good,
I couldn't believe it.
It changed everything.

Then what does it mean
to be dead, I asked. Over
and over. I really wanted to know.
You said nothing. Four
years. It was so good.
I didn't think to ask again.

Walking by Lake Harriet, I Remember Water

Seven A.M. is too early for swimmers,
except for a few people who pull along with even,
measured strokes, leaving only a thin ribbon
of disturbance. Summers growing up,
I gloried in this city green water, choking
down the occasional mouthful when jumped on
by my older brother, the holy terror in a crew
cut, while the beautiful lifeguards reigned
in white, disinterested chairs six feet up.

Through the years, some children have been grabbed
down by cramps or other invisible hands, their hair
suspended luxurious as seaweed.
I am picturing the couple who lost a son
in this lake one summer. When the dragging
boats finally quit, they would trace the shore
entirely each evening and again at the first
light on the calm waves.

My brother now saves people's souls.
In two weeks, he will marry his first couple.
I'm not convinced it will be legal. He can baptize
also—the hand cupping the white cloth over the nose
and mouth, the other pressed in the grooves
of the vertebrae like a glove, the body released.
So many kinds of death. But, of course, the believers
always return, rivulets hurrying around the ears, dark
hair pressed against the skull, the whole body
glistening, saying, *look at me, this is my life now.*

Kindness

For John Sytsma

I thought of last summer
and the huckleberries today,

how beyond boundaries of town
and road, we hunkered over weeds,

brush, scruff pine two hours
for two quarts, you telling

stories of every August you remember,
our hands singing

the simple pearls into the bucket.
We bore the heat, laughing,

complaining about our backs, saying
nothing about my leaving so

absorbed in the *thick, thick* of plucking
berries, clusters of hucks destined for pie,

cobbler, ice cream or lifted
to our mouths by stained fingers.

It was that good. John,
I am remembering the morning

of the berries, the winds
that sound like pure

loneliness on a mountain
and the amount of kindness

one man's hand can really hold, amazed at
the hungers that draw us so far away.

Phoning Home

Tonight over the phone, I told Felicia the cat thing proved
her co-dependency with her neurotic roommate. "If the cat
won't leave you alone," I said, "Just lock him in Debbie's room
until she comes home." Finally, she agrees, jostling the phone
as she stashes him. In the process, the phone goes deaf

and she no longer hears me and hangs up. I call back. She knows
it's me, but still can't hear so she agonizes on about how this is
her punishment for torturing the cat and it's Debbie's
phone too and she had half a dozen people to call tonight and
am I still there. Meanwhile, I'm screaming

"FELICIA, CAN YOU HEAR ME? IS THIS A JOKE? CAN YOU HEAR?
After 30 seconds, she's had enough of her point of view on the world
and hangs up again with me in mid CAN YOU—A new problem enters
our lives. Technology no longer surprises me. Life no longer
surprises me. It's late January and I'm realizing my most

powerful poetry is only written three days before my period
when the flare of PMS sparks through my body. Most violent crimes
by women are committed at this point in their cycle. I could be
in prison right now. Instead, I write passionate, insightful poetry
and then cry the rest of the night over the guy who cut me off

on the highway earlier. While Jan grew up, her mother had the most
bizarre way to refer to it. She would ask, "Has your little red-haired
grandmother come to visit?" Nothing can astonish me in January,
although another war erupted last week, but that's not really astonishing
if you know the first thing about America. Everywhere people

say things like "It's unbelievable isn't it? It's all so unreal.
Terrible . . . just terrible." I can't stand it. Somehow, voicing
my feelings only trivializes the enormity of it for me.
Sometimes, I think America is using a phone with the earpiece
on the fritz. It's dangerous to look like you're listening when

you're only talking to yourself, because it ends up your own voice
is always the answer. I want to figure out how to phone up
America, say the one word that would fix everything. Instead,
I'm trying to listen here in my living room on the plaid couch
with the soft light and the order of living alone, calmer now,

waiting for the next piece of news from the world,
ready to hear a good ending, anything that might surprise me.

Home of the Brave

No one else out this morning, too soon before sunrise. Running by Lake Calhoun, I note the sub-zero air is gone for now, leaving a sleepy plate of blue ice, tucked in by the blue glow of snow, shore lights vague in fog. It is quiet except for the sizzle of cars on the parkway and my shoes crunching the snowy path like breakfast cereal. The new war began two days ago and now the last one is a strange bubble rising. Vietnam was like a dark coat I wore all during childhood, a ten pound weight held so close to me I didn't know myself without it, couldn't understand my new equilibrium when it first lifted away. In Calhoun, the fish are stupid with the cold, but they don't mind the ice, the pockets of air sustain them. I can't imagine what ice would be like in the desert. An incredible, unique coldness. Most of the soldiers are not ice. Most of the soldiers are still breathing. My lungs toughen like leather by January for these runs. It will be foggy all day, fog like a ceiling of ice. The frozen lake will not change for months and the fish will grow weary of the moody, understated light. I tend to internalize war and don't feel the need to talk about it any more than I would the removal of a deep sliver in my hand, digging up my own wordless flesh with a needle, fluffing bits of skin to coax out the shaft. You don't talk, you just do it, get through. Simple. This is what you do when your father soldiers an unpopular war and you watch your mother navigate the long ocean of nightmares alone. Once she received a telegram and it took her twenty minutes to open it. It only announced a baby somewhere. She cried the rest of the day. I know the soldiers are hot. The bombs they drop burn and burn, but they are thinking about ice, some of them are ice. The furnace in my chest sweats through the blue sweatshirt, the blue that shakes through the fog, the ice, the ice that burns my face, faces burning into the ice. Beneath the ice, the fish are surprised to see the soldiers, jealous of their wide, lidless eyes. But, see, even the fish are shouting to them, *look, your life is on fire,* but the soldiers don't reply. *Tell them no,* I say, *no.* Nobody hears. I'm still running, it's all in my head. I couldn't stop the last war either. I sent sticks of Doublemint gum to my father in Saigon, I guess because they were flat and light. It was something I could do. Kelly was my best friend. Her dad was the only survivor of a tank brigade, but badly burned in all that fire and heat-keeping metal. He wore shorts sometimes when barbecuing with his *It's best in Texas* T-shirt on. The damaged skin looked like it was a hundred years old, tight and ill-fitting. Translucent almost. Kelly said she heard him scream at night. His body was never his again. During that war, my mother customized Civil War songs for us to sing around the piano:

When Daddy comes marching home again, hurrah, hurrah
when Daddy comes marching home again, hurrah, hurrah,
Judy will sing and John will shout and Janice she'll be sure
to turn out and we'll all feel glad when Daddy comes marching home.

The piano has been moved half a dozen times since then. Mostly, she plays Welsh hymns now. As I round the west edge of Calhoun, January feels ugly and unending, the exact middle of winter. There's nothing I can do about the cold, the fish, the soldiers, except to think how startling it must be when your life ices over, the thin margin of air you came to count on suddenly unavailable, the weightless fog of the body. Tendons in my legs tighten and relax in rhythm with my breathing, which is not endless, but is warm for today. It is calm on the path. It is calmer with the blue light of the fish. The soldiers with them are indistinguishable from the ice except for their faces, the openness of the open palms. They still love their families, this thing called America. They have already forgiven us. It is the only way to get through.

Last Party at Zarzyski's Place

For Paul

Forget the whiskey mornings of Butte,
rodeos in prophetic places like Great
Falls, and the poems that shut
down in Missoula, Montana, there's plenty
of pie and beer and Patsy Cline
is dead serious tonight about *heartaches,*
heartaches, my lovin' you meant only
heartaches, so pass her a brew
and a handful of pretzels. Tired
of broncs that had you for breakfast
and cities that fenced you inside,
you're packing it up for Santa Fe or Santa
anywhere, but here, life in more fragments
than you thought possible when pounding
the back door of thirty. Even Patsy,
both dead and serious, is three sheets to the wind
and pining in the corner, *I fall to pieces*
(oo wa oo) each time I see you again,
so mournful, the moon cries over
the rabbit hutch in back. But come
3 A.M. in the kitchen, you jitterbug
with a girl who's seen fifteen fewer winters
who could love you, her long hair
a rich brown you can't name except it is the color
of horses you have ridden. Swinging her across
linoleum, your first place silver rodeo buckle
flashes, polished all night
with the wild, reflecting sweep of her face.

Letters to My Sister

Having driven halfway up the Al-Can
highway in a '69 Volkswagon, he dumped
you. Not for anyone else,
just for you, but you continued north
to find cannery work for the first time,
propelled by stubborn,
living scar tissue alone, your new
address as vague as your plans:
General Delivery, Alaska. It feels
as though I'm mailing letters to thin,
cold air with my younger sister's name
attached. Between us,
we have built a hundred staircases
to regret. This new one no less mine.
Nonetheless, your postcards arrive:
Valdez is a hellhole. I leave
for Ninilchik in the morning.

When you chugged for the end
zone during that touch football
game years ago after a Hail
Mary pass, I gave chase, diving
for your legs in a last
ditch, unethical tackle that sent
us both sprawling, mostly you,
effectively stripping the skin
from your knees. I am thinking
of the blood swelling over the wounds
speckled with hard,
dry November dirt.

Gutting fish eighteen hours a day
in the high season, you write:

I know the tendonitis is getting
bad when I lay in the tent at night
and can't feel my arms. And I can
only reply, *come home,* amazed
when I think how much of our lives
as children are spent disowning
each other. Soon, it will be September,
I visualize Ninilchik turning its face
toward winter, slowly roping in
the slack of unending light.

There is this dream I have
about two children arguing
until their words burn holes
in the air. Finally, the words scream
across their pink skin. The fire
awakens me. I remember your knees
took weeks to heal. I understand it now:
I couldn't stand for you to outrun
me, even that one time.

This is the letter where
I tell you everything: you were not
dumped on our doorstep just before
dawn in the gray-blue light
of late winter, or discovered,
bundled and crying, anywhere near
our mailbox. You were not

an accident, your real mother
and father wanted you all along.
Sister, you are one of us, please
believe me, please respond
right away, make me certain
of your forgiveness.

For Mary About to Visit Minnesota during Sweet Corn Season

I'm warning you now. There's a delicate,
pearl-yellow ear for every mountain
in Montana. You'll notice the train
will tug like an impatient dog on a leash
across North Dakota, make no stops
after Bismarck. They know.
Our menus are planned: sweet corn
and cole slaw, sweet corn and Ken's
Firehouse Beans, corn and potatoes,
corn with toast, corn with corn, unshucked
ears smoldering on the barbeque,
fingers of smoke important
as a new pope. You will have difficulty
sleeping at first. This is normal.
Don't worry, there will be three salt shakers
on the table at all times. And butter,
yes enough to grease your chin indefinitely
and plaster the tiny kernel hearts
to your cheek like the kiss
of a fabulous celebrity you'll vow
never to wash off. I'm telling you
all this beforehand. Your room
is ready. Better bring winter clothes.
The kettle is on to boil.

What Is Left

It amazes me how a hunting dog
can be so fearful of thunderstorms,
but there she is curling up beside
the stove a few feet from where I work
in the kitchen. This spring afternoon
has sunk to a greenish dusk, the third
and worst day of rain. The vet says
she won't see another season, the lumps
like small, wrathful cities multiplying
across her belly. But this fear
does not touch her and she still
eats well, the soft flaps of her ears
perk at the smallest kindness. Finally
dozing, her paws do a jig, signaling
a dream: her nose is full of the one
pheasant she will never retrieve.
No matter how quietly she stalks
and points, and bird stirs early,
cracking the blank October sky.
I prepare the evening meal, thinking
of the fields that are left: the ones
we walk when there is no rain
or just after and the ones farther off
which we will also walk in the proper season.

Thinking of the Peaches

For Carolyn Thompson

That was the summer of the bruised peaches
when you and I both got jobs at the natural food
grocery in Missoula, Montana, $4.50 an hour
and mostly broke in our blue aprons, cutting
boxes, stocking shelves, ringing up organics
for yuppies, hippies, and occasional transients.
You drove the Cro-Magnon Renault with T-shirts
for seat covers while I cruised on my black
three speed permanently in third after the gear
shift fell off. At closing, we'd rummage through
the "free to staff" boxes filled with limp
carrots, puckered cukes, worn out romaine.

In July, the peaches arrived. The damaged, the
dropped, the jostled, the worm-nipped, the kid-
thwapped were up for grabs. A peach in the hand
for lunch, a plate of peaches for dinner,
the season was so short and we couldn't get
enough. The first bite was loveliest, opening
the shine of so much sweetness all at once.

They went with us everywhere. Swimming
the Blackfoot on Sundays after church, a brown
bag of peaches nested in the sand. Or driving
up Garnet Mountain to the ghost town, picnicking
among the miners' cabins that leaned with bear
grass, aching for collapse. Then,
at season's close, the settling of August,
sitting on stools in the back of the store
talking at shift's end. Sore feet and peaches.

Carolyn, I am writing this to say I am thinking of
the peaches and how nothing else has ever tasted
that good, to tell you I've never had so much for free.

The Last Spill of Light

LANGUAGE IS THE ARCHITECT OF SMALL COMFORTS . . .

Dogs in Flight

Twenty-eight and back in Minneapolis, answering phones for
executives I've never met, talking to people I'll never see,
familiar with their office names: Milt, Kathy, three Karens,
Jim, Jody, pulling America's motor vehicle
records out of a computer like rabbits out of hats.
And the other office girls (who really are girls) wander
the wreckage of failed relationships and talk
of marrying into whatever isn't this. I am half-specter,
half-participant. Twenty-eight years old and back
in Minneapolis to "help" my writing, I must've been nuts,
living at home again where my mother shopped the Target sale
today and has bought me a three year supply of Kotex.
I need to get beyond this depression. I need to find my footing.
In my bedroom tonight, writing by the light of a lamp
I actually own, I know it isn't the office, the girls,
the tightassed city living, or even all the Kotex I had to clear
off the bed. It's about how I won't let go. I am thinking
of the dog I had when I was twelve—how he would
clench a towel we'd tussle over and I'd work to wrench
it back. Once, I started swinging him around, unaware
of the possible danger his unclamping in
mid-swing could bring, only knowing he never did let go
and only now wondering if the flight meant anything to him,
his front legs tucking toward body, the spaniel ears folded
back like small, brown banners, the prize fraying away
from his teeth. Finally, I gave in, slowing him to a tumble
across the soft lawn where he rose and shook himself,
stumbling dizzy for the first time in his life.

The Myth of Other Lives

Over the phone, Teresa is describing her aquarium with disgust:
wait, my crab just came out. Three bucks and I never see him.
Then, there's the gourami fish—five each and they always have a foot-
long string of poop hanging underneath. I'm tempted to flush them
or give them to the cat in a Cool Whip container. I'm listening
to this, it is Friday night. I did the club after work, had leftover
tofu for dinner, then poetry. Then, Teresa's call interrupting, but

the words were in the dumper anyway. Sometimes, poetry is like
synchronized swimming which I saw in the last Olympics. Sure it
takes a great deal of precision, skill and dedication, but why?
Teresa's aquarium is the size of an Oldsmobile. She loves the endless
quality of underwater life, the myth of other lives. But, it's never
like we plan is it? It's so easy to forget that some fish carry
their crap with them. Maybe it's what she feeds them. Sometimes,

I wish I were a fish, the kind with sleek racing stripes that illumine
tropical waters, darting their small bodies in the beautiful traffic
of coral and other exotic animals. My eyes would never close.
I would be so perfect. I would never live in a bowl. Each day spent
spanning the blue water, my lovely gills would billow with molecules
of oxygen, synchronized with a single thought of living: *breathe,*
breathe, then I would simply go on, juggling the universe.

The Aerobic Instructor's Body

The shining lycra giftwraps thighs, breasts,
midsection, each color applauding the magnificent
course. We mirror her every move, strain
to match her reflection, arm for arm,
ankle for ankle. Everything good
in the seen world gathers into
her body, muscles beautiful and obedient
as dolphins, pumping lungs, the treasure
that weighs us down. A weight that is
not envy, but the danger of believing
the light falling from her body,
the submission to the unattainable.
In the pounding music we are thinking
about the slow flame of fatigue moistening
our faces, the powerful absences
of our bodies. We fling ourselves into
the vision, the dream: the instructor smiling
back when we face our own mirrors,
suddenly laden with the beautiful,
utterly translated, our skin shining.

China Letters

For Mary McVee

In the beginning, it was easy, you wrote, *I have finally*
mastered riding a bike in China. Today, I nearly ran
over a chicken. I love my students. I will
enjoy teaching here. I said, *I have decided to leave Missoula,*

I cry about it daily, but I know it's best, remembering
your warnings: *be careful in your letters, our mail is opened.*
Lately, I have seen the clips of Tiananmen Square, children
singing songs of home, the troubled sleep

of a thousand hunger strikers. I have seen
the trucks of frightened peasant soldiers
and the fists of the government shouting. Mary, I remember
your stories of teaching the students to decorate

a Christmas tree and how a skewed translation
instructed them to glue not tape the stockings
to your wall. For the first time, I matched the faces
in the paper with those eagerly

crowding your apartment after class and my sudden guilt
surprised me, overwhelming as a forgotten continent.
I can't be silent any longer. I need to tell
you all the times I have read headlines for entertainment

and stared at photos of people's tragedies
with mere interest. Tonight, on the evening news,
I saw the masses in the square, soldiers, the bloody
faces of students in the last lurching

frames before the blackout, the return to the newscaster's
face. Suddenly, I wanted to weep unceasingly for a billion people,
touch each of them on the shoulder and say, *please forgive me.*
If I start now, I might accomplish this one thing.

This is the letter I read to you every night
from America so I won't forget, so I will say
everything when I see you again. Still, your letters,
sealed and re-sealed, arrive: *The climate here*

has turned for the worse and *I must visit you next summer*
to explain it. I say, *I am writing down a few pieces of my life.*

Happiness

What's left of the day spreads
into a thin layer of light across
the lake's far shore. Now, the moon
has come. A dinner plate laid quietly on a table.
The dark water becomes darker and
we all begin to bundle our things for home.
On the dock, people have fished all evening. A couple
of them are into metal slamming from a boom box and
wear Harley Davidson T-shirts, crappies
on a stringer. A kid unleashes
a sunnie and loses it like a bar of soap
on the planks where it tap dances
back into the lake. I sit dangling
my legs over the dark city water imagining
the Laotians next to me are laughing over
some good fortune, a gold coin they will find
in the mouth of the next perch. The woman
wears a flat straw hat and a long blouse
as if she is returning home to
a lush jungle of orchids,
the immense comfort of custom. Mostly,
there are children lured by an old wish
to remember how to breathe underwater.
They have dreams about it sometimes and
it's easy. It is a secret lung each of us has
tucked deep inside our chests. At the right
moment, it will unfurl and receive the water
and when we have had enough of such happiness
it will, like certain flowers, simply
close its ravishing petal for the night.

This Town that Takes the Series

> "This town needed a win. I'm glad
> for the town."
> —*Kirby Puckett, centerfielder,*
> *Minnesota Twins, 1987*

This town can't find a seat
on the Lake Street bus and loses
a shoe on the escalator at Dayton's,
this town that chalks up nosebleeds
in crowded elevators suddenly
one October pitches pure nerve
with a holy right arm and plunges under
every cage-faced catcher's tag at home.
It's this town that is the Minneapolis boy
in a two hundred slump at bat with the bags
loaded in the sixth. See how nothing
matches the beauty of those yard
wide shoulders cracking the pitch
and the wallop of tension
as the ball scales the roof, arcs
in a slo-mo calm, descending into one
meteor stitched with our names
for a bleachered riot of hometown underdog
free-for-all, desperate to roll Volkswagons
and kiss complete strangers. Watch this
town rounding first in a clatter far beyond
score and dazzle, trotting the bases
slow enough to hold onto the thousand
decibel brawl tearing every ear drum,
the bedlam of a million white banners
beating down all odds against, leaving
one town wild with our own good luck.

The Basil

Every evening I water the basil,
patient leaves billow
like curves of the heart,

grateful.
I sit near them a while
breathing that one fragrance

like another country.
They remind me
I cannot help but pray

when even one city street
is overwhelming, the thick elbows
of sorrow endless. Grass folds

back into sleep, the calm yard, large
bodies of trees cradle
the last spill of light.

I wear this sadness like a jacket,
but this song
is for the garden, for everything

that can be named by my nose
as the cool kneels down over us.
The basil, nourished in damp soil, is ready

to begin again. In the summer
of troubles, I touch
the wide generous leaves

that soft perfume,
a heart I am still grateful for.

For Instance, a Woman on the Brink

> "I don't believe in ultimate things, I
> don't believe in the inextinguishable
> light of the other world."
> —*Edward Hirsch*

From the 35H downtown bus, I watch
the huddled lumber of morning
rush hour, headlights strung
together like beads for miles,
haloed through humid windows in
a wash of business suits sectioned
off by briefcases. I believe

in ultimate things, but let's face it,
some things are more eternal
than others. I think: *I am going to work*
and it is still dark, as if I am
the only one burdened with this,
when I return, it will also be dark.
The ways of God are unsearchable,
but I'm unsure what this means
just now, except to say, sit back
it could be a long ride,

the outlines of cars stenciled
on the darkening face of autumn.
I survived the summer that went
badly, now what? Where does it come
from, the blood necessary to do this
day after day? Marching into downtown
amid this dull parade, what if

the bus exploded right now?
I don't think this world is ever
enough—not the vanity
of buildings competing with the sky
like Babylon squared, not the curb
reaching up in gray comment from
the street—and the first evidence
of this is poetry, that fierce bread
feeding us enough to go on
in our hunger, to wait for our stop
and step down finally in departure,
to simply continue.

Mercy

Today at the health club in the 5:00 rush to push
muscle, all the handicapped parking spaces were taken
by non-handicapped cars. I felt a gallon of blood flash
into my head, my brain a mallet about to pummel something
and, without thinking, I called 911. First time ever.
I even gave my name. I spent my workout waiting

for the intercom voice to page: "Will the woman who
called the cops on the handicapped parking violators
please come to the front desk. The owner of a red mustang
wants to beat your face in." I concentrated on the weight
machines, adding plates until my triceps burned through
to my elbows. I never showered so casually in my life.

But as I dressed, I felt calmer. I did the right thing. This week,
I've been haunted by the stoplight I ran the other night, alone,
half glancing at the map riding next to me, the red noticed
like a sudden anger in the unfamiliar intersection. My legs
disowned me in seconds, all the electricity of fear collecting
there until they were heavy and foreign. The cross street

was clear. I'm thinking about being totally blameworthy,
yet unpunished, how the one time we glance away can be
either meaningless or change destiny. I'm learning about mercy—
giving it or not, receiving it or not. Walking toward my car,
nylon bag slung over one shoulder, the sun still holds steady,
the light bearing the weight of everything undeserved.

Looking for Work

My Reeboks muddle the uneasy expanse of Harriet beach.
I can list the things I'm afraid of on one hand and what
happened today is not among them. 7:15. Darkness comes
so early in October. Sitting on the floating dock dusted
with sand near the white skeletons of life
guard chairs, I watch the cars rounding the lake,
how the canes of reflected headlights on the water lead
each one toward some thought of destination.
The first cold snap catches in my bare hands. The soft,
blue lining of my jacket hunches up around my neck.
I can still see the man in the suit full of excuses at
the office saying, *this is why it is,* who watched my angry
voice shake across the room. For ten minutes, I was the angel
of justice, fabulous with rage. Now, I wait for the momentum
of the thing to come upon me. I thought: *so this is what it means*
to be principled. It could be a lean Christmas. Something
in this life drives me—God, vision, ego—all at once
and from nowhere. I am looking for work, some place
uneventful, where I can lean my heart for a while and do
simply with my hands, begin the calm reassembly of this corner
of my life. The dock will be here all winter, brittled
with bits of lake weed. The pocked sand cups its share of shadow.
Small lights far across Harriet ride like feathers the dark water,
searching for rest, goodness, one last thing to praise.

The Rain of Leaving

Believe me when I tell you
I drowned last night.
Sitting on the curb today,
waiting for a bus in a downpour,
I smell your beard
in the dark flaps of leaves
deep as orchids around my head.
The cold drizzle
of your name beads my lips,
eases down my chin before
the blind burst to ground.

This water belongs to me now.
It will trickle down my shoulders
and slip into my lungs forever.
The air, weighted hard with November,
perfumes itself with the exhaust
of late busses, the ghost-breath
of those that never arrive.
Listen to me. My rain-creased face
is the map to a cold country.
But, look, love, how in my pocket
I have saved the first
terrible bloom of your smile.

Still Life #9, without Fruit

1.
In the beginning, someone
tied a note around the truth
and heaved it through
every window in town
and called it poetry.
Later on,
the way the shards
gleamed
across the floor
determined
whether it was art.

2.
In group, Guy was feeling bad because
it was really difficult for him when he had
to visit his parents in Akron for five days.
Janet said she couldn't live
with anyone for five days,
except maybe God and then
only if he kept all his promises.

3.
The lilacs I picked reign on the kitchen table,
a rich purple foam fat with light and air.
Each benevolent column leans away from the jar,
acknowledging endless cheers from the peasants.
This is the first day. Tomorrow, a few petals
fall, pale on mahogany and the peasants begin planning
the revolt. The story is about art and perfection, but
I'm not supposed to tell you that. It is all an illusion.

We can only own different endings, perhaps another
village in a strange country with a five syllable
name that stumbles across your tongue. There, the people
work the land, perspiration sprouting around the hairs
on their temples. To them, dropped petals are a gift,
the blessing of an open hand on the forehead.
They have no time to peel back the mirror. It is harvest,
the first spark of light is on the wheat.
Long blades wade through the fields, the sun climbs
between their shoulders, the story they know.

4.
A letter on the chair arm
from John in Albany, Oregon:
I still greatly miss you. I'm trying
to explain how this year
has gone with all the wide
ranges of emotions and struggle . . .

5.
I was showing these photos I took
to Felicia. There were some really good
ones of her. She stared at them,
disappointment scrubbed across her face,
do I really look like this? Well, yes.
She shook her head, *then I'm not cute.*

6.
Today, I noticed there is this despair
in every aisle of Rainbow Foods and within
minutes I'm carting it around.

It grows larger and larger. Then, I've
actually got to pay someone for it
and hang it in plastic bags off my arms while
I waddle to the parking lot. And, of course,
it's raining. Wet despair. Fine. Don't think
for a minute this is a metaphor
for one damn thing, except what it is.
Don't read it again,
it's not art, it's just Wednesday.

7.
Is this really what you mean to say?
The reader has to make too many leaps.
It just doesn't flow well and I'm not
sure the peasant thing in number 3 is working.
Dissect your heart again.

The True Meaning of Soup

For Betsy

After almost quitting my job,
my anger discharging
like a rifle for two days,
after wandering all evening,
a ghost in my own apartment,
I pick up the gift
you gave me today,
the illustrated Book of Soups.
There is something

soothing about Watercress Consommé,
Harvest Barley, Rosemary and Lentil,
or Chicken Noodle, that old
yellow mitten of childhood.
And then I remember my grandmother:
only those who love enough
make good soup. Gazpacho,
Soup Georgette, Hungarian
Cabbage, each photographed

in bowls beautiful as the moon
with thin strips of carrot,
pasta big as a bell,
the delicate hands
of parsley reaching from
four cups chicken broth,
two eggs, the juice

of one lemon. I am carefully
measuring out everything now.
This is the moon
of comfort, the moon of order.
I want something that simmers,
a circle of warmth in my
stomach all night.

Grandma, look, I am boiling
the meat like you said,
the onion is ready,
I am learning how to love.

The Architect

I'm thinking of words,
of how one thing always references
another and must
if we are to understand at all.
Today, I am angry with my life
which is really to say
I have little or no control
over the runaway car of events
parked on a hill, innocently enough,
the brake disengaged, tires inching
into a roll. The car

tumbles over curbs, shrubs,
fences, takes on a life
of its own, it even has memory.
It remembers me sitting
at a job I merely endure,
driving home in October with
the lights on, macaroni and cheese
for dinner. It sees
sadness, careens toward
the weighted heart.

Car is a word the same as *sorrow,*
each of them takes me someplace,
however unexpected. I am speaking
of my life, the one story referencing
one thing, then another,
and eventually all things. Language
is the architect of small comforts,
willing to trace the sometimes terrible
velocity of our lives, the empty
steering wheel, every reason
I can think of to just go on.

"Muscles" Hougen Comes Out of Softball Retirement

Years ago, I was so lovely
at second, diving for the fly in the ninth,
kneecaps pounding packed infield in a hard
tumble, raising a pregnant glove above
my dust-spackled body. A play so solid, you could
display it on a coffee table in your head
for days. My left hand is again an elephant
ear of old leather, a set of hot dog
bun fingers shined dark and smooth in spots from
a thousand line drives to right snagged
on the bounce or plucked like an overdue apple
from flight. These days, it's difficult to cash in
my body for trophies. The nights are long,
hot baths, and "Liniment" Hougen
smells more and more like my true name.
With my knees two small buckets
of pain, I stalk the base line, spit
for effect, crouch down with palms against
patella and wait the play at second
that's still second nature. Right foot
on the bag, left arm stretching
for the grass-streaked splendor of the ball
swacked to right, I brace for it,
lean every bone toward the catch,
the chance for one thick
leather hand to reach into that much beauty.

The Center of Gravity

It has taken me years to understand this,
how I can go to bed and everything's fine
and wake up invading Panama, to understand
my science teacher's words about the center
of gravity: *that point through which the resultant*
of gravitational forces on a body passes.
I barely made it through remedial geometry,
physics out of the question, but I know
centrifugal, scattered from axis, my nose
in the paper, my body at the movies. It's
December. I've always imagined the center
of gravity as the last place left when all else
fails, somewhere near the bottom of the world.
Tonight, I think I invented propulsion,
my eyes are on the freeway, windshield
smeared, twenty below, washerfluid frozen.
It's like driving on bedrock in a tin can,
the road a narrow hallway to nowhere.
I've flirted with the edge, with gravity,
that fierce, last love, the one eternal
attraction, the place we all tumble to when
we have tired of swinging around the family
dog on the soft lawn all morning. Arms locked
in a dizzy world splintered with grass spinning
around us, we see things properly
for the first time, find it at last: axis, home.

The Length of the World as We Know It

REDEMPTION SHOULD BE SO ORDINARY,
LIKE WALKING OR MAILING A LETTER
TO A CLOSE FRIEND . . .

The Mirror

A thirty-year-old woman
has climbed into
my face. I am not
alarmed, but
she is unclear about what
she wants. Her nose
is burned from
softball, her shoulders
ache, her mouth
tastes like poverty.

It's not what I meant
to notice.

I'm beginning to think
my morning shower
is rusting
my joints.
Afterwards,
a hair-thin
lake of water
covers the mirror.

Some mornings
the woman
comes to me
and says, *it's getting*
late, everything
eventually subtracts.

I interrupt the glass,
write a few suggestions
across the dark
stones of her eyes:
live, live, live.

The History of Fish

Clearing the clouds, sun smacking the wing,
angling across my face, I settle into my seat
on the noon flight to Salt Lake, transferring

to Seattle. Already bored and useless,
I glance at the beautiful magazine photo
of tropical fish in the lap next to me, each one

the brilliant flag of its own small nation, delicacies
amid the blunt hands of coral. You could get lost
in that sleepy, green light. In grade school,

we studied fish that glow like bright stones
on the bottom of the ocean. *Glowfish Tetra.*
I imagined the phosphorous fins cutting dark,

comforting the watery night like a bed lamp.
Years later, on television, I saw small fish
trapped in underwater caves which had lived

entirely without light for eons, their bodies adapting,
eyes like two wounds healed over by darkness. I saw
the scientist's flashlight hit the blind, twisting bodies

shining in his palm, filmy membranes bulging
from unused sockets. It is strange to make these comparisons
now, miles above any water, the clatter of the lunch cart

edging up the aisle. From here, I'm guessing
we've both been soaked in darkness a long time.
But don't we long for our lives to resemble this wind

of steady, unturbulent light? I want to remember
everything important about today: the tidy lunch,
the history of fish, the fearful and precious

potential of our lives. The sun fires fields of clouds,
burning into its own horizon. A thousand eyes couldn't
hold it all. Look at it with me. What hasn't light taught us?

The Dream that at Once Fills and Empties

How it Begins

In the dream, the eyes
green, blue

legions of the dead

they have come
to lift the weight

it is all there
open your hands

to say for one moment

remind you
the fixed eyes

mother, father
change into rain

The Sign

It is all there
to lift the weight

they have come
legions of the dead

green, blue
in the dream, the eyes

change into rain
mother, father

the fixed eyes
to remind you

to say for one moment
open your hands

The Length of the World As We Know It

From the produce section, I notice you in the check out line
as I finger McIntosh, Jonathans, the last sad cantaloupe
no one in their right mind would rescue. You say hello
after paying, we talk about mutual friends, church,
as if to build a reason for a man and a woman
to hold a conversation in a food co-op.

I sometimes say to new acquaintances, *fundraising*
is my Clark Kent job, my real life is writing poetry,
and gauge the future of our relationship on
their response. Today, I want to tell you,
your face could live in my hands a long time,
or *I would rearrange my life for you.*

You talk about your little boy, the single
parent support group. Every word I speak
tastes like cotton. Sometimes I want to risk
handing over an important piece of my heart
right away, reveal the wonderful, precarious ways
we travel the length of the world as we know it.

Instead, my defenses stay latched. We probably
won't stumble across each other again for months.
After you bundle your bag to your chest and go,
I thumb grapefruit, heft a few in my hands.
They would look beautiful in my basket.
I am hungry for that pink that tenders with yellow.

The Front Page

> "A grieving father reached out to caress his
> dead child, lying among a row of corpses in
> Chittagong, Bangladesh."
> —*photo caption*

The 6:30 alarm opens a day of possibility,
the morning run threading through sewer repair,

early traffic, the expensive, black-fenced
cemetery my grandmother is buried in.

Breakfast is plain yogurt and brown rice cereal.
The paper says maybe 100,000 dead in Bangladesh,

although the photo is of one man, five dead children.
A single grief. The man reaches toward the row of

children. I can't tell which one is his, can't see him
gathering the body a second later, holding it, dressing

his own child in the pure cloth of sorrow. Taking some
time off from work, I'm wearing my favorite oversized

sweatshirt, looking for a pen. This morning,
I don't understand how I'm supposed to live.

Bach's *Brandenberg Concerto* floods the living room,
I review pages of notes. How should my life be different?

What else can I do, but embrace this quilt
of normalcy, continue on quietly, just as I've planned?

Enough

That was long ago, pausing
on the Higgins Street bridge,
clumps of smoke standing above paper
mill stacks, no heavier than air
or lighter, small hands that said, *this*
is your serenity, take it now. I did
or at least I tried, I can't remember
now. I asked you, *you've lived here*
all your life, how can smoke say such
things? It was the middle of summer,
the absolute, best time to be living
in Missoula, the dust and light scooped
by legions of pigeons roosting on top
of the Wilma Building. Small gusts
of wind from passing cars billowed against
our backs, the last degree of shadow
possible today, August 3, lingering
behind us. It was enough, the wonderful
hover of smoke holding what light
remained, a peace offered unexpectedly
with both hands, the gentle traffic
of birds sliding through dust and light
as if air were something they created.

Inner City Youth Center

Crying, the nine-year-old finally broke
and told everything. Heather, her youth worker, said
the surprising part was not the beatings, but that

her mother refused to feed her. The girl spoke of it,
that's my mom's food and lived on school lunches
and snacks at the center. We both know a call from

Child Protection would likely trigger a new level
of bruises and solve nothing. *Sometimes my mom
buys me cereal, but she always ends up eating it herself.*

Heather has some things to sort out. I tell her to
just do what she can. When Jesus said, *In this world
you will have trouble,* he meant for the children,

the dispossessed, those trying to help. Of course, there
will be new disasters to move through, other children
wandering the asphalt, nightmares rolling

behind their eyes the old movie called "Annihilation,"
starring someone they love better than their own hands.
The bright, red meat of their wounds is endless everyday.

In this world you will have trouble. For today,
we bless the women who loved themselves enough to feed us,
grateful to be nourished, still here, doing what we can.

Can Anything New Be Said about the Moon's Highway of Light across Water?

See how things converge:
the night my Toyota
is smashed while I sleep, a woman
I know is nearly killed in a car accident
in Montana. They have removed a pane
of her skull to allow
the swelling brain to breathe, to exit
like an angry neighbor.

My reckless sleep that night
surfaced into a long wail of wheels,
crushing metal that instantly belongs
to me. The next morning, I found
the driver's door caved in toward
a vague thought of my body. This evening,

I hold fast to my life with two grateful arms,
stride the solid proof of my existence,
the flesh still knit around my bones.
I remind myself the soul is stronger

than anything, but I am sick of strength.
Across the water, the moon glazes
a path to my door, delivering a thin refuge
of light in its silvery hands,
something for the long drive home.

Once You Have Removed God

At first, you must
remind yourself
daily, paste
yellow notes
to the refrigerator
bathroom mirror,
other strategic

places. Let it be
the first
thing you see
each morning. Make
lists with every
third item: *don't forget*
to remain an atheist.

Okay, so maybe
the hole
shaped
for the burning
face of God
has closed over or
filled with the long
nightmare
of your father's likeness.

It is what
it always is,

vacancy:

an aluminum boat
on a gray lake
in September,

the old leather
suitcase left
in the train station
of a country
you only planned
to pass through once.

One More Day

Thumbing through my parents'
Saturday mail, I discover the only letter
they've opened thus far is from the Cremation
Society of Minnesota. The envelope sits near
the pamphlet, *Cancer Facts for Men,* a preventative
publication, but unsettling. How long does it go on: roast
beef for Sunday dinner with the TV news, cinnamon

apple sauce and asparagus, maybe a run
with the dogs later? Channel 5 reports on a recall
of Sudafed due to two deaths in Washington.
We discover the bad lot number matches
my parent's box. Dad's mouth is open, he's struggling
to remember when he last took some. Mom
pretends to faint face-first into her applesauce.

I say, *I think you would've known by now,*
trying to be helpful. Another brush with at least
the thought of death. It is more frequent now.
The winter labors, leaving glazed concrete
under the morning paper that dulls into watery
afternoons. The footing is never certain. We clear
the dishes and Dad slips beef scraps to the Brittany

camped under the table, warranting a daily scolding
from his wife. Mom pours the coffee and I pass date-filled
cookies, the white dough sleeping over the dark,
sweet paste. What is it to sit here on an early
March afternoon with this benign couple in their mid-sixties?
It is one more day, the open blessing of the ordinary,
and we are all here, drinking it together.

The Snow Scene Bottle

After fifteen days of rain, the sun
has saddled the sky again, cottonwoods
throwing handfuls of themselves into

the sudden summer air and, for the first
time in years, everyone's luck is real.
In your car at the parkway intersection,

fluff is snowing everywhere—on people
waiting for the light, in gutters, across
the brilliant grass—announcing,

yes the day is manna, eat your fill now.
It's like heartbeats of light tumbling
across your dashboard, like the snow scene

you bought when you were eight at the Mississippi
headwaters, plastic flakes lazy in the dome
of water turned over again and again

to coat the tiny family on their amazing
vacation. Snow that is never
cold is a celebration in the palm of your hand,

the sweepstakes you've entered all your life
and now the line of cars, the dizzy confetti
is a parade in your honor. Wait the green light,

find a forward gear. The radio says,
everything gets reborn if you'd only ask.
The seeds spangle like acrobats,

you could be mayor and this your election party.
Drive into it, hold the wheel like that elegant
toy, the child will not stop for hours.

Half the Story

Under the harsh, fluorescing light of sixth grade,
we all exchanged photos, Mr. Gullickson
offering two different pictures of himself. I chose
the one of him wearing the confident, white
turtleneck, because it made him look less
like a teacher, more like someone who could
save your life. That was grade school, the dead

serious notetaking of relationships in the final
year of the war, colors of the flag striping
the edges of envelopes from my father in Saigon.
At recess, I watched Mr. Gullickson while waiting
in line for my turn at four square, lost in the science of
those brick-red rubber balls. I sat spellbound when he
read us *Stuart Little* and cried quietly at my desk

about the dog buried at the end of *Where the Red Fern Grows.*
When a trip to Taylor's Falls was announced for winners
of our class paper drive, sacks of the *Minneapolis Star*
were stacked like bullion in the back of the garage. I bicycled
around the neighborhood Saturday mornings, rummaging
through trash for stray newsprint. The neighbors thought
I was nuts. I collected ten times more than anyone.

Mr. Gullickson, I needed you because I didn't
know myself well enough yet to say, *beautiful.*
When the teasing of other kids became my textbook
for self-esteem, I retreated into rooms where I was noticed
and important, not the awkward girl about to become
doubly so with adolescence, that odd time spent
in the back seat of my life while my body

drove where it willed. Listen, I still have the Instamatic
photos from Taylor's Falls in my pink picture album.
This is you by the rest area near dusk and the ride home.
This is me sitting on the wall, the canyon rising across
my back, clutching the rough stones into the camera's single
memory, my eyes writing down ideas of a woman, quietly
seated near the end of a story, lovely beyond imagination.

Self Portrait, 1991

Friday, Felicia said, *of course Rose is jealous,*
you've got your life in order, all your ducks in a row.

The thought surprised me. After the excess, the fury,
the broken axis, it is strange to land on this time

that balances, leaves few regrets and keeps
the bottom of my refrigerator clean. I run three miles,

sip coffee, and read the morning paper over yogurt.
I have signed up for church softball. I sprawl

across my couch, trying to write more. I go to my weekly
twelve step. *All your ducks in a row.* There are days

I like to stand at my dining room windows and survey
the sewer repair three floors down on 35th Street.

Branches nod and leaf in a cloudy May chill
that makes me useless. I want it to be enough,

to be right. Spring is the slowest season there is.
Someone somewhere mows their lawn,

the sound grinding through the window glass.
Redemption should be so ordinary,

like walking or mailing a letter to a close friend.
The hard-budded branches still lift an arm

of greeting and I am standing here in a small gap
of my life, finally remembering how to wave back.

Poem for My Parents' 45th Anniversary

We dig at ice cream and store-bought sheet cake,
signaling cards, packages, family clatter loud
as bright paper and camera flash. All of us
circle the dining room, passing the mixed nuts,
a cousin refilling coffee mugs.

I count everyone
who would be missing without the pretty receptionist
encountering the returning GI in the Federal
Reserve Bank who stood up his uncle
to have lunch with her. Tonight, the table
is surrounded with testimonies to this good fortune.
The latest addition, my brother's child,
has found her legs with authority, our own little
stormtrooper of the carpet.

At mid-sixty,
they watch marriages split by death, hardly knowing
what to say, the one partner dazed and amputated.
It reminds them they have no solid memory
of a life apart, how more and more in the middle
of the night, one will tense till the sheet pulses
with the other's breathing.

Mom says, *I don't want*
you kids spending money on us, while Dad tilts
his head slightly to funnel the conversation into
his good ear. Parents who think our lives so complex,
their existence simple as yes on a June night
in 1946, lost in a warm breeze from the porch screen,
with barely one thought of these familiar faces
invented since then, the large, comfortable light of family.

Fitness Club: Riding the Lifecycle

"We're as fat as we are dishonest."
—*Judi Hollis*

The control panel counts time, calories, miles
gone, outlining hills to come, the red lights
beating calmly, saying, *the place you need to go*
is at least 15 pounds from here, how willing

are you?, mile after mile. I could have pedaled
these phantom wheels across America by now.
Anchored to this amputee of the modern age,
I give away the last thickness of fat to computerized

inclines, to a blinding honesty that must negotiate
with everything I see. After years of struggling through
a life fed by half-truths, I am laying down the past like
the careful molasses of asphalt: a thick, methodical

roadway. It doesn't solve everything, but it's real.
I am willing to hold the sad weight of every lie
I told while raging at the world through my body.
These days, movement is no longer

optional. I have learned to welcome
the sanity of each mile, to love the woman
inside this engine who reinvents the wheel
daily and now has important places to go.

Judith Hougen was born in Alaska in 1960, the middle child of a career Army officer. She received her B.A. from Bethel College and her M.F.A. in poetry from the University of Montana in 1987. She is the recipient of the 1990 Loft-McKnight Award and a 1992-93 winner of the Loft Mentor Series. Her poetry has appeared in various magazines such as *Indiana Review, Georgia Review, Kansas Quarterly* and the *Nebraska Review,* and the anthologies, *The Origin of Tigers* and *The Perimeter of Light: Writing about the Vietnam War.* She lives in Minneapolis, Minnesota.